Dr. William R. Morgan

The Real Stuff of
SUCCESS

finding success and significance in life

TATE PUBLISHING & *Enterprises*

Content-Development Editor: g. Susan Wilt

The opinions expressed by the author are not necessarily those of Tate Publishing, LLC.

Published by Tate Publishing & Enterprises, LLC
127 E. Trade Center Terrace | Mustang, Oklahoma 73064 USA
1.888.361.9473 | www.tatepublishing.com

Tate Publishing is committed to excellence in the publishing industry. The company reflects the philosophy established by the founders, based on Psalm 68:11,
"The Lord gave the word and great was the company of those who published it."

Book design copyright © 2008 by Tate Publishing, LLC. All rights reserved.
Cover design by Nathan Harmony
Interior design by Summer Floyd-Harvey

Published in the United States of America

ISBN: 978-1-60696-271-8
1. Motivation-Self Help-Business Ethics
2. Dentistry-General
08.10.13

What's Being Said in the Dental Community

Dr. Bill Morgan is one of the most amazing dentists I have ever met. In fact, he is one the most amazing men I have ever met. His genuine love and care for people and dentistry shows in these pages of *The Real Stuff of Success*. I am excited to see someone like Dr. Morgan care enough to share his vast knowledge with the community. His book is packed full of information and if you choose to put it to work, it will certainly change your personal as well as your professional life. His true commitment to serving others is his path to "real success".

Sue Marshall, Coach
Director of Coaching
The Coaching Center (Dental Boot Kamp)

The Real Stuff of Success is a concise and practical portrait of the hard-earned development of a successful dental practice. I have known Bill Morgan for many years, and his life is an authentic model of the principles he develops in this book. Bill correctly argues that true success is borne out of character and relational commitment, and that excellence in the service of others is the path to true wisdom.

Kenneth Boa
President, Reflections Ministries, Atlanta, GA
President, Trinity House Publishers, Atlanta, GA
Ph.D., New York University
D.Phil., University of Oxford, Oxford, England

Dedication

I want to dedicate this book to those I am most thankful for. First to my beautiful wife, Laverne, who has stood by my side through all the hard years of our journey. She has managed our household well and is the loving mother of our three wonderful children, Missy, Mark and Brad, and grandmother of our eight beautiful grandchildren. Secondly, to my mother and father, Ilene and John Tillman Morgan, who loved me enough to instill good core values in me. They sacrificed for me and encouraged me to go to college and dental school, a privilege no other Morgan had experienced until then. Thirdly, to my dental mentors, Dr. Charles E. Stuart, Dr. Pete Dawson, and Dr. Bill Dickerson; the teaching of these three men daily influence the care I give my patients. Fourthly, to my spiritual mentors, Dr. Ken Boa and Dr. Dave DeWitt, who have guided me, encouraged me and challenged me in my spiritual journey. And lastly, but foremost, to our wonderful God and Creator who is the giver of every good gift.

TABLE OF CONTENTS

Chapter I: the Early Years of Struggle | 19

A brief chronicle of my early years of struggle to establish my practice and operate profitably; realizing that the formulation of a basic philosophy of life and correlating mission statement would need to be established if one is to lead not only a financially successful life, but a life of significance.

Chapter II: Philosophy and Mission Statement | 23

How one's philosophy of life and mission statement relate to success in dentistry; to have a successful business, one must have core values which will lead to significance and satisfy life's most basic question: "Why we were created?"

Chapter III: the Staff | 29

How to have a productive, highly effective staff meetings; Your staff is your best asset; The importance of hiring, retaining and leading the right office staff; Characteristics of excellent office staff; How to hire and retain a staff that will support your business goals; Sharing your philosophy of life and mission with your staff. Getting everyone on the same page; Building trust within the team; Motivating the staff; Effective and productive staff meetings; The perils of a passive resistor on staff; Correcting staffing mistakes; Setting Goals; Improving Systems; Improving Relationships; Staff Training; The importance of attending continuing education seminars; Staff bonding; Planning fun staff events; Ask the staff; Staff is the key to enjoying and having fun in your practice. Staff compensation–how to do profit sharing and how it will benefit you.

Chapter IV: the Patient/Client | 49

Developing a trusting patient-base that not only accepts treatment but will refer patients; how to handle patient fear from the first phone call through the operatory experience.

Chapter V: the Dentist | 61

Self-assessment, beginning the journey to success; what sector do you want to serve? Keys to success–Attitude, Pride in work, Continuing Education and Time Management.

FOREWORD

There are two ways you can acquire knowledge in life. The first is by attending the School of Hard Knocks. You do learn important lessons there, but it takes a long time, and the experience is painful and expensive. This book is important because it presents the second way to acquire knowledge, by *modeling,* a way of learning from other people's experience. Modeling is quicker and much less painful and expensive than the School of Hard Knocks.

Most dentists work because they *have to.* After many years in dentistry, Bill Morgan practices dentistry because he *wants to.* Most dentists dread walking in their office doors. Bill Morgan strides into his office with a smile. Bill will be an excellent model for you. In his many years of dental practice, Bill has seen it all. He's struggled. He's made mistakes, small and large. But through it all, he kept improving and refining until he created and crafted a practice and a life that exemplify *The Real Stuff of Success.*

When I first met Bill Morgan at the Las Vegas Institute for Advanced Dental Studies in 2001 I noticed right away there was something different about the guy. We began a conversation that grew into a friendship. When he asked me to write the foreword for his book, I jumped at the chance. In this remarkable book, you will discover not only how to make your dental practice more successful, but how to design a practice that is actually an enjoyable part of your life. Some of the things Bill shares will be revelations, while others will be reminders. Either way, you will harvest and profit from the experience of a man who has discovered *The Real Stuff of Success.*

American novelist, Kurt Vonnegut, wrote, "New knowledge is the most valuable commodity on earth. The more truth we have to work with, the richer we become." Bill's book is packed full of the simple truths that will make you rich–*spiritually, emotionally and financially.* Read it with great care. Highlight the ideas that resonate with you. *Then implement the knowledge in your practice and life. You will be glad you did.*

Nate Booth DDS, MS

Author of the books *Tiger Traits, The Diamond Touch, Thriving on Change, Let the Chips Fall Where They May;* and co-author of the books 555 *Ways to Reward Your Dental Team, How to Create an Exceptional Aesthetic Practice, Unleashing the Power of Dentistry, Change Your Smile, Change Your Life* and *Change Your Bite, Change Your Life*

A man that has been at both ends of the dental marketing spectrum writes The Real Stuff of Success. He managed a low fee dental clinic making quality dentures and he managed a high fee dental practice that treated the whole patient with few appointments. Both services are needed in serving the dental community..but..if you are a young dentist getting your practice started this would be an excellent book to help you decide which type of dentistry you wish to pursue. If you are a mid-age dentist looking to change the way you practice… then this book will show you how to take your practice and produce the type of dentistry that best suits you. Dr. Bill points out that partners who are quality thinking and really want to serve people are essential to the "Real Stuff." God has driven Bill and his partners to be held accountable to themselves as well as Biblical principals that always produce "The Real Stuff of Success." Read this book and grow as a member of the dental profession.

Dr. Alfred L. Heller, DDS MS
Director, Midwest Implant Institute
Author, Teacher of 28 years, Father, Grandfather, Husband of
50 years

Dr. Bill Morgan has put together a wonderful account of his lifetime of experience in developing a rewarding practice centered on patient care. Bill has highlighted the important aspects to succeed in this difficult profession we call dentistry. But more than that, Bill has put together his philosophical beliefs to not only achieve personal inner success and happiness.

I am excited to see someone like Bill, whose thirst for knowledge and desire to be the best professional servant for his patients, cares enough to share this valuable information with others. It is my hope that his positive attitude and commitment to excellence through continuing education will infect every reader of this book.

I am proud of Bill and his prolific dedication to getting his message out give him the accolades due for the sacrifice and effort he put forth in conveying his personal vision. Our profession would be a better place if in it, it had more Bill Morgans.

William G. Dickerson, DDS, FAACD, LVIM
Founder, CEO LVI Global
www.lviglobal.com

Preface

As we labor day-to-day in our profession many of us struggle to make a decent income and enjoy the journey, we often fail to derive a real feeling of significance in our work or personal lives. Many of you have completed four years of college and graduated from dental school–no small accomplishments! I have written this book in an effort to help you find and enjoy success you deserve on your journey. I want to offer some things that have transformed my practice and life.

I want to tell you how I went from dreading going to the office every morning to loving dentistry so much that even after selling a highly-successful and growing practice I continue to work eight days a month simply because I enjoy it so much and from being so in debt that I had to borrow money to meet my personal bills each month to now enjoying a very nice lifestyle. Like most of you, I practice daily with both gnathological and functionality generated concepts, but the single most helpful thing that has enabled me to enjoy dentistry and make an excellent profit was the cosmetic and occlusion training I received at Dr. Bill Dickerson's Las Vegas Institute for Advanced Dental Studies. I also suggest some basic strategies that will make your day at the office fun as well as profitable and ways to grow a solid referring patient-base. I share my ideas on how important it is to deliberately identify a personal philosophy to guide your life and thus help you find significance in your life. I pray that each one of you will truly enjoy your years of practice, enjoy your journey and find satisfaction in your life. The journey continues!

Soli Deo Gloria

Chapter I
The Early Years of Struggle

The fact that you are reading this book says something about you. You have a desire to be more successful in your profession and your life and have perceived a need to begin the journey that will lead you to achieving that goal.

> *We don't stumble into success.*
> *We position ourselves to attain it.*

In the 70s, I had a dream about living in a beautiful home on the lake where I could enjoy a peaceful retirement and I wanted to do that by the time I was 55. I didn't fulfill the dream until I was 58–but I missed it by only three years. Even now I am not fully retired because I continue to enjoy dentistry too much.

I have reached many of my other dreams that only ten years ago seemed absolutely impossible, and the reasons and ways I achieved any success is the real stuff of what I want to share with you.

Philosophy is the reason! Philosophy is an abstract concept that may at first seem farfetched, but it is one's philosophy and beliefs that motivate us to get out of bed each morning. *And that motivation is the heart of success.* Everyone's life is motivated by something. What motivates you? As Rick Warren said in his best seller, *The Purpose Driven Life:*

> *"The way you see your life shapes your life. How you define life determines your destiny. Your perspective will*

influence how you invest your time, spend your money, use your talents, and value your relationships."

What defines success in your life? The way you visualize your life will design the path you will take. What you're seeking you will find. Visualizing yourself as being successful is the first step toward success. If you see yourself successful you will work to achieve success. When you choose to climb the ladder of success you will want to make sure that when you reach the top of the ladder that it's leaning against a wall that gives meaning and significance to your life and that when you look over the wall the view will be what you were hoping and working for. The selection of the right wall will give meaning and passion to your day-to-day living.

I am not referring only to success in dentistry—as dentists, we all want that. I'm talking about the kind of success that brings a sense of self-worth; a success without which it is difficult to find the deeper meaning of life, i.e. *Why did God create you? Why are you living on planet earth?*

To achieve the success we desire in our profession we must be sound in the basic principles of dentistry:

1. High quality technique

2. Administration of systems

3. Management of people

4. Management of finances

These are the essentials. But what compels you to achieve high quality standards in these four parts of your practice? Is it the money? Is it personal/professional recognition? Self-gratification? We all want a share of those things. But if those are the only things that form the basis of our core values, we will still find ourselves empty after achieving them.

If the French philosopher, Jean-Paul Sartre, was right when he said that there is no creator and thus we are only a product of chance, then nothing matters and life is meaningless so the only real success is living a life of hedonism. Well I've tried that and it is void of significance. Finally, I asked myself a depressing question, "Why bother with anything?" That was also Sartre's conclusion—life is meaningless. This was not a good place to be!

The real stuff of a successful life resides in our hearts. To have true peace at the end of the day is to have answered the question, "Why did my Creator create me?" When you can answer that, not only can you have success in dentistry, but in your senior years, you can look back over your life and be pleased. Not only will you have attained professional success, your whole life will have had significance. Life has a purpose that leads to significance. I found purpose and significance in life and so can you.

If we never take the time to ask and answer these philosophical questions, any success we enjoy will be temporary and without depth. I have found that success in life is meaningful only when we have significance.

Chapter II
Philosophy and Mission Statement

How is all this translated into success in dentistry? Years ago I established a philosophy and a subsequent mission statement that defined who we were as a team. For my staff, the statement clarified who I am and what I expected to achieve in the day-to-day care of my patients.

This is the philosophy we live and serve people by:

"God has brought us together as a team to serve people by improving their health.

Our desire is to provide the highest quality dentistry with care and compassion.

We have an attitude of do unto others as we would have them do unto us, for our patients and each other."

If you do not believe in God, that's your prerogative, and I respect that. But my belief in the God of the Bible is the foundation of my core values, informs my choices and moves me forward in life. I did not come to any faith until I was 29-years old. Until then, I was an agnostic. One day I decided that if the truth existed I wanted to find it. After examining the claims of Christ, I believed He is who He said He is. When I became a believer my whole perspective in life changed. My relationship to my family and friends changed. My perspective on my practice changed. Do you need to share my perspective to have success in dentistry? No. It's true that you can have success in dentistry and not be a Christian. But everyone must have core values that lead to significance. And if we are to know real peace, we must answer life's most basic question: "Why were we created?" I found my answer through Christ.

A few years after writing my philosophy statement, I followed the recommendations of Dr. Omer Reed, a well-known lecturer in dentistry from Arizona, and developed a mission statement for my profession.

Be an office in the top 10%

1. *Be committed to quality dentistry*

2. *We appreciate our patients and they appreciate our services*

3. *Our patients exhibit good dental health*

4. *Seek continuing education for constant update(to stay on the cutting edge)*

5. *Personnel paid in the top 10%-compensation*

6. *Take pride in what we do and what we are all about*

7. *Enjoy working together-HAVE FUN!!*

8. *Use the best equipment available*

9. *Be in the top 5% in cosmetics*

You might ask *"Why should I listen to Bill Morgan?"* Good question. Let me tell you about my professional and personal life-journey.

In 1957 my high school graduating class in northern Indiana had high ideals. We would make the world a better place of peace, prosperity and good will for all—have one big group hug, light a candle, and sing the Coca-Cola song. But perhaps like yours, my life was a more practical series of events: college, US Navy, marriage, family and dental practice. It was a practice of trial and error, ups and downs. Maybe like yours is now. But my practice was growing and I had monetary success.

In the late 1970s I experienced severe back problems common to dentists and thought my wet fingered days were over. At that time, dental lecturer and consultant, Avrom King of Arizona was expounding his future vision of dentistry composed of three tiers:

Tier I - Ideal Practice

1. Seeing fewer patients than the average practice

2. High fee dentistry

3. Not insurance driven

4. Using the latest technology

Tier II - Clinic Dentistry

1. Insurance driven practice

2. High volume practice

3. Low fee

4. Basic dentistry techniques

Tier III - Salaried Dentistry

1. Military dentists

2. Dentists hired by large companies to treat their employees

At that time, Sears wanted to place dental offices inside their stores nationwide and one of their representatives contacted me in Knoxville, Tennessee and wanted me to open their first dental office in the South. Because of my back problems that seemed like the best thing for me to do and so I entered that Tier II market. It would prove to be an error in judgment. I believed I could hire dentists and deliver high-quality dentistry using low fees and high volume. Many dentists today are still trying to do this and it's a mistake! Something must be sacrificed and if you want to make a profit–it's quality. At Sears, I hired some great dentists and delivered quality but with no profit. This situation prompted me to "clarify my head and heart" as Avrom King said we must do. We have to decide which market we want to serve.

There is nothing wrong with serving this much-needed market with the basic services of dentistry. These people need our care. The point is you must decide which market you want to serve and if that's the market you want to serve, that's fine. But it's not as profitable unless you are willing to work longer hours and many days per month.

That experience caused me to focus both my head and my heart and make some changes in my life. The key words here are *focus* and *change*. As a result, the great dentists on my Sears staff became my partners in private practice. In 1988 we severed our ties with Sears and built a state of-the-art dental facility. We had some hard times at first as all new businesses have, but we had developed a quality dentistry mentality grounded in a philosophy of delivering the highest quality dental services to our patients and as a result experienced phenomenal growth using only internal marketing. Our fees became some of the highest in the area.

At Sears, our office was open twelve hours each day, six days per week. After my move from a Tier II philosophy at Sears to a Tier I philosophy in our present location, my practice morphed into what I believe to be the ideal practice for me. My team and I saw patients only 11 ½ days per month and work six hours a day and yet produce far more than most practices produce in double the number of days. We almost always have our lunch hour on time and finish at 4:00 p.m. If this sounds good to you, read on.[1]

> ***The secret to my success is in the core values of what I have determined to be important in my life.***

This is the real stuff of success.

A patient who returned to our practice after having left because of our high fees shared the following story with me:

As a manager of a business, one of his salesmen gave him a business card with the following maxim:

> *"Quality, Price and Service-Pick any two and I can deliver it"*

The point is this–*You can't deliver all three.* You must decide who you are and which of the two you want to deliver. Only then can you have the kind of success I am talking about. This patient and many others returned to my practice because they wanted quality care and service even though the fees were higher.

Chapter III
The Staff

**The most important asset you have to help
you achieve success is your staff.**

Your success or failure will largely depend on how your
staff responds to your patients. Staff members who are
stuck in neutral and are simply putting in their time
will suck up your profit in their paychecks. Even one
passive resistor will have a negative effect on an entire
team dedicated to helping you achieve your goals. I call
this Staff Infection! Imagine a team of five astronauts;
four are on the same page and one is stuck in neutral, just biding time! Who could depend on him/her?
Columbia to Earth ... HELLO! Get rid of the passive
resistor. A few years ago, I had a lazy assistant who was
a passive resistor and honestly, if she had been working
on an incline she would have been sliding backward. If
you have a dream to achieve, get rid of the bad apple
quickly! One bad staff member can destroy the whole
team. I've kept bad apples until the whole team started
to reek. I have learned the hard way.

Unless you write out your dream or goals on paper
and share them with your staff, your staff will not have
a clear focus and will lack direction. They may be a
great staff, but they won't know who you are or what
you are trying to achieve. Step up! Be a leader! This
comes back to core values; decide who you are and
define your goals. When you've done that, let your team

in on it. Give them an opportunity to get on the same page with you. It's vitally important that they know and share your vision. If a team member doesn't buy into your goals and you can't help them see the rationale of your direction, you must get a new team player.

You are going to need a great team if you are to achieve your goals. Most offices call their staff a team, but is it really a team? What constitutes a great team? First, they must also have core values that include truth, honesty, a willingness to work, a quality dentistry mentality and a desire to do the right thing in every situation. And they must first see these qualities in you. These are the qualities of an individual who is above the norm and could succeed in many occupations. Oh yes–they are hard to find, but they're out there and you can find them if you look. The kind of people I'm talking about must be paid well, yet money is not the force that drives them to do their best. They will want to be appreciated and respected and to please both you and the patients whom they serve. If money is your staff's driving force it will stress you greatly. If money is your driving force, both your staff and your patients will know it. When a patient comes in with a chipped tooth that could be fixed long term with something other than a crown, it is a moment of truth and an opportunity. How you deal with this patient will define your truth. If you always do what is best for the patient, the staff will observe that quality in you and it will set an example for them to follow when responding to your patients. This is the way you form the high quality staff that you want them to be. The patient will observe that quality in you and their trust and confidence in you will grow. Years ago Dr. Earl Estep, a nationally known dental lecturer from Athens, Texas and a classmate of mine from dental school, said it in a way that has stayed with me: "Don't eat your seed corn. It will all come back to bear fruit if you plant the seeds."

The staff must be able to *trust* you and they will begin to build trust when they observe your ethics you exemplify in the daily, moment-by-moment decisions you make. They will learn to trust you to always to do what is right and best–not just for yourself–but for your patients and them.

The primary core value of a team is trust.

Doing what is right originates from the core values of who *you* are. Do I always make the right decisions? No. But as soon as I realize that I've made a bad choice, I apologize and try to make amends. Apologizing may build more trust than anything else I do. Saying "I was wrong" may be very difficult to say, but try it. It gets easier. I know because I had to learn to say it, too. And when the occasion arises your spouse will appreciate your ability to admit that you were wrong as well. I have been married to Laverne for thirty-nine years and have had to eat a lot of crow. Want a good recipe for cooked crow?

Staff Compensation

I know what it's like when there's not enough money left at the end of the month for personal expenses and during this time staff compensation suffered. All small businesses go through phases where the dollars needed and wanted are just not there. The first step to financial stability and success is to *stop overspending in your personal life,* and the second step is to *get out of debt.* I went through a period when I had to borrow money to feed my spending habits and it was a tough time for Laverne and me, but we survived and prospered, and you and your family can too. (Debt will be addressed more fully in the chapter on Dental Economics.)

Profit Sharing is the best way to motivate your staff to help you achieve your goals. It will be good for the whole team. Begin by analyzing the overhead in your office and comparing the percentage of your collection that you pay your staff with national/regional averages. Make sure your numbers are in line with the averages. When I first started doing this, the national average of cost for the entire staff was 22% to 23% and I was right on target. My aggregate staff salary for the year was 22%. I looked at the break-even point for the total overhead for the month. When you know what it costs you to practice each month, decide on a fair target compensation salary to pay yourself at that monthly production. Notice I said FAIR. That doesn't mean you soak up all the profits.

If you have a high accounts receivable it will eat your profit!

Profit sharing will motivate your staff in a big way! I implemented a profit sharing plan designed by one of my partners, Dr. Jim McKinney. This plan would give the staff 25% of all collections after we–the dentist and staff–had earned our base pay. For example, for each $1000 over our target goal (the amount determined by our monthly overhead plus my pay), the staff received $250.00 to divide evenly among themselves, and I received $750.00. This is fair since the doctor has invested all the dollars, time and effort in establishing the practice and takes all the risk. With profit sharing, the staff knows that any increase in production, efficiency and collections will bring the staff rewards.[2]

Each staff member is an essential person on the team and should share the bonus evenly based on the number of days they worked in our practice. Notice I said *our* practice; that is the value I instilled in my staff. When the staff feels that it's their practice as well as yours, they will help you build the practice. With this type of system the staff becomes highly motivated and becomes very interested in controlling overhead because *they do not get raises—they can increase their compensation only with increases in collections.* They were so motivated that they provided the momentum I needed to be even more productive.

I did not raise my pay or the staff's individual pay. The increases we all enjoyed were due to our increases in production and collections. The bonus for the staff was paid at the end of each quarter to average our bad months with the good. At the end of the year, we averaged the year so in the end they received 25% of our collections. I never get burned by bonus if we had a month that I lost money and then if we made bonus the next month, it was always averaged out.

With this bonus system, if I wanted to take days off, I could do so and it would not affect their pay as long as we made our production/collection goals each month. Yes, this happened regularly with proper time management along with proper staff motivation, but office efficiency is not the subject of this book. They would make less in their guaranteed daily pay since we worked less days, but they always made the same or more by making our monthly goals. They loved it! They worked less and made more. So did I. With this system no one was unhappy or walking around on eggshells because they knew they were being well paid and treated fairly. This system created such a fun, happy, well motivated staff that my job became a dream. The daily grind was gone because the atmosphere in our office was fun, and the patients saw this every day.

My wife and I got a free cruise to the Caribbean each winter because of my motivated staff. Several years ago, I was analyzing my year end numbers and noticed that we had only produced $4000 in teeth whitening. I think you would agree that most of your patients would love to have whiter teeth. This is the age of cosmetic dentistry so capitalize on it! I told the staff that if we reached $15,000 in whitening sales we would use 50% ($7500) to buy cruise and airline tickets for them. We started in January and reached our goal by August. At that time $1500 bought a 7 day cruise with a little extra spending money for each of them. The following January, my wife and I along with five staff members enjoyed a winter getaway on board the *Golden Princess* sailing to islands where the sun is warm and the palm trees sway. It did not cost me anything since it was found money. We did that every year! We raised that to $1600 per person and $16,000 in whitening sales. Talk about a staff motivator! They got in the habit of talking to people about the color of their teeth and my whitening sales increased to $20,000—so we all made more money. To make the trip a legitimate tax deduction, we held onboard staff meetings using Dr. Nate Booth's video seminar, *The Yes System.* It was Nate who inspired me to write this book and even gave me the title of the book, *The Real Stuff of Success.* [3]

Implementing the whitening idea increased profits and staff benefits which in combination with the compensation plan made it practically impossible for another dentist to take my wonderful staff from me.

Money is not the primary motivator of an excellent office team. However, the money must be there to hire and keep quality people. The primary motivator for a quality staff is a sense of self-worth based upon real accomplishments, recognized and affirmed by you. The staff needs to know that they can freely offer their suggestions regarding the direction of the practice and that you will listen to and respect their input. The staff wants and deserves to be respected and to know that they are valued members of the practice and that you have their best interests at heart.

Assets

A competent and loyal staff is your *greatest asset* and will greatly influence if not determine whether or not you have a successful and profitable practice! They acquire valuable information while interfacing with your patients and are in constant touch with the pulse of your practice. Be wise and *listen* to them. Using the business strategies I am sharing with you, my yearly production skyrocketed. My practice achieved tremendous growth while working less days–*only 11 ½ per month,* and decreasing daily hours–*working only six hours per day.* Suddenly I found myself enjoying dentistry again!

Having the right staff is crucial. Hiring and keeping the right people and the proper management of those people are critical to the growth and continued success of your practice.

When searching for a new team member, the composition of your ad in the Classifieds must be distinctive and stand out from the others. Avoid all the usual clichés such as "progressive, busy office". Begin with a bold heading such as:

"DENTAL ASSISTANT", "DENTAL HYGIENIST", or "DENTAL PRACTICE COORDINATOR"

A Dental Practice Coordinator is much more than a receptionist; she is the quarterback of the team. Word it something like this: "Exceptional opportunity to be a part of a fun team". Because I am proud of the reputation of our team and practice I always include my name and address in the ad.

After the resumes come in, I select the best ones and have my Practice Coordinator call the selected candidates to schedule a personal interview with me. The initial interview usually takes about half an hour and after the initial interviews, I choose the two best candidates and schedule a lunch interview for them with the office staff. I do not attend, but of course I pick up the tab. After the lunch interview, I confer with the staff and listen carefully to their evaluations because they are able to provide insights that we as dentists may not have the time and opportunity to observe. The staff will quickly weed out the average candidates. They will never suggest someone they think won't hold up their end of the work load because they have a vested interest in the efficiency and productivity of the team. And they won't recommend anyone whose personality they believe is incompatible. Finally, I have the staff's selected candidate come in for a third interview and if all goes well I extend an offer of employment.

Listen to your staff. One day I was walking down the hall to the conference room to conduct a first interview when one of my staff members passed me in the hall shaking her head "No". She was right from the start. Listen!

Dealing with Staff Problems

I have found that the best way to keep inter-office problems to a minimum is to have regular one-on-one meetings with each staff member. In these meetings, I ask each one of them how they feel about their position and their relationship with the other staff members. I ask if they are having any problems in the office carrying out their duties. I also share candidly and truthfully my assessment of their job performance. If there is an area that needs improvement, I address it and clearly state the changes I expect and give them a definitive timeframe in which I expect it to be resolved. The salient points of these meetings are documented and placed in the employee's record to refer to in future progress evaluations. The staff knows we will be having these one-on-one talks about their performance regularly and they don't particularly enjoy these meetings. However, when the meetings are over, most often they are feeling good about their work as it is a unique opportunity for me to express my appreciation of the fine work they're doing and how much I enjoy working with them. If there are any areas of concern or potential problems developing they can be addressed promptly and adjustments can be made before the practice suffers any setbacks. Don't wait for a problem to surface and have a meeting to confront it. Schedule regular one-on-one meetings during the year so that everyone knows when it will be.

When problems are brought out into the open no one has to walk around on egg shells; there is no silent hostility brewing; everyone is happier and the work goes well. The cooperation and harmony in the office is obvious to patients and they often comment on the pleasant and friendly atmosphere in our office. This is a practice builder! If you do have a team member who is not capable or willing to be a real team member, let that person go so they can look for an opportunity in another office where they can fit in and be happy.

The passive resistor will kill your practice. This person may, on the surface appear to be a cooperative employee, but behind the scenes she gossips, causes trouble among the other staff and fails to carry out your requests. When you identify a passive resistor you should part company. If she/he fails to respond properly in the one-on-one meeting, inform her of her termination, give her two-week severance pay and ask for the office key. A team member who is not capable or willing to be a real part of team should be let go so they can look for another office where they can fit in and be happy. It will make you very happy that she/he is no longer there and the other staff members will most likely be relieved too and affirm that you made the right decision. Remember, with their vested interest in their paycheck, they too want an office that flows smoothly and is steadily increasing in production and collections.

Staff meetings

In most offices, both doctors and staff hate staff meetings as they tend to turn into gripe sessions. However, because of the profit sharing, staff meetings can be very uplifting and positive because everyone wants the practice to be better and to grow. My staff knows that I want to be the best dentist I can be and that I wanted them to be the best professionals they could be. If someone doesn't want to do their best to achieve our set goals they do not belong on the team and are in the wrong office. Let them leave and find the right place to put in their time.

The purposes of the staff meetings are to:

1. keep us on the same page

2. improve office efficiency

3. increase the quality of our service

4. get staff ideas

5. create staff bonding

6. upgrade staff training

7. increase staff motivation

8. set goals

The following are some ***ideas you can use*** in staff meetings to help you achieve these goals.

1. *Develop Your Philosophy:*

Write an office philosophy statement that will shape and guide the personality of your practice. It should reflect core values that define who you are and what you are trying to accomplish with your life and set the standard in how you care for your patients. When you have an awareness and a vision of your purpose and destiny, communicate that to your staff in your philosophy statement so they will have a good understanding of who you are and what you expect from them. In practical daily application it will guide them in treating your patients with the same care, skill and judgment as you do. They will treat people the way they would like to be treated which is the heart of good customer service and it reaps dividends not only in income, but more importantly, adds significance to life.

My office philosophy:

"God has brought us together to serve people by improving their health. Our desire is to provide the highest quality dentistry with care and compassion. We have an attitude of do unto others as we would have them do unto us for both our patients and each other."

This philosophy was developed in a staff meeting in the 1970s and we discuss it periodically to maintain focus and reaffirm commitment.

2. *Staff Motivation:*

Discuss motivational articles written about highly successful service industries such as Ritz Carlton's philosophy of service. You might want to bring in a successful local business professional that shares your values and have him/her give some of their secrets of their success. This will motivate you as well as your staff. Make the meetings fun.

3. *Set Goals:*

Create a realistic vision for your team by setting yearly, monthly and daily production goals. Review and discuss your present production and collection numbers with the staff. This can be a little scary unless you have put together a "real team." There is trust in a real team that allows the dentist and staff to support each other. Maybe you're thinking that this would never work. But it has been done and is being done and yes—it will work for you. But you must have the correct mindset and the right staff. When you are able to involve the staff in the production, collection and overhead of the practice they know approximately what you make. But it will fine with them if they are getting their fair share from the profit sharing as described earlier. When you reach this level where everyone can trust each other you are smoking! You are a real team! I never revealed how much each staff member made and they understood that different levels of education and experience were factored into each ones' remuneration. Each of them earns a fair wage for their position yet all participated and shared equally in the bonus system depending on the number of days worked and thus are very interested in the goals you set.

True trust within a real team will make your life wonderful and you practice fun because everyone is working for the same goal. Give your staff an opportunity to get on board and they will because it gives them a vested interest into your practice. You must provide the leadership and give direction but they can help with the formulation of ideas. *Ask them, "What do we need to do or change to achieve our goals?"* Then listen to them! Bring them in on the planning stage and when you have a written goal that that everyone can support and achieve–it will happen!

4. *Improve Systems:*

Addressing the areas of communication within the team will improve office production, efficiency and staff relationships. For example, in our office, the handoff of the patient from the assistant to the practice coordinator needed improvement because people were leaving without scheduling the next appointment. We changed the system so that the assistant uses the operatory computer and sets that appointment. Another example is–if your hygiene numbers are down get their thoughts on the recall system you are using.

5. *Improve Relationships:*

In a light spirit of fun we took the DISC personality test so that we could understand each other better. This did help us to understand each other better and it allowed us to cut each other some slack and the intra-office relationships improved. During one staff meeting, I asked each staff member to write three nice things about each of the other staff members but not share the notes until the next staff meeting. When we shared them it was great and the end result was like a big group hug singing "Kumbaya". You talk about a highly oiled efficient fun team—we had one! I know it sounds corny but it's highly effective when we are dealing truthfully with each other. Would it always remain that way? NO! The intra-office relationships are always changing. Like any important relationship we want to grow, it takes an investment in time and creativity. And yes—this takes effort and energy. But the dividends are fantastic. It brings joy to the practice which will go a long way in reducing office turnover.

Office turnover decreases efficiency and causes a huge loss of income.

6. *Staff Training:*

This is a great time to train the staff on some new techniques. The team could practice patient-response approaches in role play—like how to ask that great patient for a referral of their friends.

7. *Seminars:*

When you and your staff return from a seminar take some time to discuss and evaluate the possibility of implementing some of the ideas and set a timetable in which the changes will take place. The team could read dental articles or books and discuss them for both personal and practice growth. When we grow personally we bring more to the workplace so everyone benefits.

8. *Camaraderie:*

A well-bonded staff will make your day at the office more fun and a great deal easier. Here are some things you might want to do to encourage camaraderie–when you have the right team. Every staff birthday I would take the whole team to the restaurant of their choice for lunch. We scheduled a long, hour and a-half lunch to make sure we didn't run over in our schedule. It is important that each staff member be recognized and celebrated on their special day. Unless this time is reserved and honored we will miss the opportunity to celebrate that person.

When you make the team the priority, good staff members will not take advantage of you.

For Christmas and Hanukah we drew names to exchange presents. I selected a nice restaurant for a party and we took the entire afternoon off to celebrate the holiday and enjoy each other's company. We drew names during a staff meeting but kept the names secret. A list with everyone's name was posted in the lab and each person put what they wanted on the list. The camaraderie was great! One year, Kathy Finn, a great hygienist, who loved to play games with us, listed different types of lingerie items under her name because the entire team knew that I had her name. I didn't know they knew so they worked it for a lot of laughs!

You get the idea! The bonding and fun often begin when we drew the names and continued until we had our office party.

The Road Race. The staff planned this one. We divided into teams of two people to a car and had a scavenger hunt to find items that were hidden or chosen throughout the city. Each team had a team name with costumes to match such as red necks or runaway brides. We caused several stares as we entered *Victoria's Secret* to get an item on the list. The finish line was a restaurant where we had dinner and gave 1st and 2nd place prizes. We did this on a workday afternoon and the staff received their pay as usual. Yes, it costs money, but the benefits include a highly motivated staff that wants to reach your goals as well as theirs. Everyone benefited and everyone had fun. This can be done with one or two other fun dental offices.

One afternoon we played laser tag. The staff wasn't told ahead of time. They thought we were having a staff meeting, but instead we went to play laser tag. Lots and lots of laughs! This kind of fun helps to create a very healthy team spirit. You might want to partner with another dental office that you know would be compatible. More people, more laughs, more fun plus build relationships.

During one staff meeting, we took an impromptu road trip when President Bush was in town. When the staff meeting started, I yelled, "Road trip!" We piled into my hygienist's van and headed out. We had a Dutch treat lunch and great fun. They were paid for the road trip. But with profit sharing it didn't cost me anything because our production for the month did not go down.

Other ideas you might want to use: an after work pumpkin carving contest at Halloween or holiday office decorating party at Christmas—and have pizza delivered. If you live in a football town have a tailgate party and potluck dinner. Be sure to invite spouses otherwise you will find yourself in the doghouse–trust me!

9. *Ask the Staff:*

Ask the staff to identify areas of the practice that could benefit from improvement because they often see things that we might overlook. This may sound scary, but remember–if you have a team built on trust they will want to make things better. You don't have to implement everything they suggest. You are the leader and thus you will be the one making the decisions for the team. But you must honestly consider the value of their suggestions. They are a great resource. Be brave and ask them!

Scheduling and Structuring of Staff Meetings: In order to have quality time with the staff you *must* schedule time for the meetings and keeping your commitment reflects the importance you place on your staff and their development. If you try to squeeze it in between patients or during the staff lunch break it won't be productive–it will be counterproductive. It will be crowded out by your patient schedule and/or the team members trying to squeeze in a bite of lunch. The failure to schedule and honor the time dedicated to a staff meeting will convey that you do not value them, the team or practice improvement–and their perception will be correct.

Depending upon the need, I scheduled an all-day or a half-day meeting once or twice a month. We scheduled a meeting every January to update and set the agenda for the entire year.

Staff meetings are not gripe sessions. If you have a problem with anyone on the staff it should be addressed in private in a one-on-one meeting.

Staff meetings should be fun and not dreaded. We began our meetings with some uplifting thoughts and/or with a reading of some verses from the Bible.

In a staff meeting, participation by everyone on the team is important. It is *not* a time for a doctor lecture or monologue as that would undermine what you have hoped to achieve. Encourage every team member to express his/her thoughts and opinions. Draw them out by asking leading, non-threatening questions and then listen to them. Let them know that you value their input. I always considered their suggestions. But at the end of the day, they knew that the buck stopped with me. I had to make the decisions and they looked to me to be the leader. This is one of the things I learned from my team–they just wanted to know and feel like I had listened and heard their ideas. Think of your staff meeting as a board meeting with the leaders of your company and get them involved.

There are many creative things you can do that will improve the way the office *feels* to your patients. Patients can sense the camaraderie in your office and will comment on it. One of our patients, a psychologist who works in business group dynamics, gave my staff rave reviews and compliments. And I did too on a regular basis–because they deserved it!

Has my staff always been great? Certainly not! But for over 10 years my staff was wonderful and there were peak periods before the beginning of those ten great years. The group dynamics change so it is constantly a work-in-progress. However your peace of mind and your profitability is worth the effort.

Many years ago I experienced what I have come to refer to as "Black Wednesday". It was the worst day of my life. My office was not running smoothly and there was much backbiting behind the scenes. One of my great assistants told me that she was resigning and that I should fire everyone else. I failed to listen. Then another employee told me I needed to fire everyone. Still I didn't listen. Then a former assistant came to fill in as a temp and at the end of the day she asked if she could speak to me before she left for the day. When we spoke, she said, "You need to fire everyone on your staff." I am a slow learner, but I heard this former trusted assistant and friend. The next day, I cancelled all patient appointments. On Black Wednesday morning when the staff reported for work, I asked them all to have a seat in the reception area. One-by-one I called them in and let them go. Difficult? You bet! I hate confrontation but it had to be done. When I called my receptionist in, I got a surprise. When I asked her how I had handled things, she replied, "If you don't want to know, don't ask." She was right on target and brave enough to offer me constructive criticism. She said that I should have fired everyone six months earlier and that I really should learn something about management. She was fantastic at her job but had gotten caught up in the dynamics of a bad office. Fifteen years later another great practice coordinator (receptionist in dental vernacular) turned in her notice and who should appear and apply for the position? The receptionist that I had fired on Black Wednesday! She and I still had a trusting relationship in spite of Black Wednesday. I rehired her immediately and was thankful to get her back! I know this may sound like a soap opera but it happened just that way. Long story short, we were all blessed.

The saga that began with "Black Wednesday" illustrates how sometimes things are not so great and changes must be made. You already know that the toughest part of a dental practice is staff management. The staff can be your best asset or your worst nightmare, so all the effort you expend to create a winning team—"The Team" is going to be worth it.

> *The creation of your ideal team will not happen by accident. Rather it must be intentionally formed using good people skills and leadership.*

To enjoy the whole enchilada of success you're going to have to assemble a really great team. My staff relationships were not instantly perfect. And yes, we still did things that hurt each others' feelings. But is this not true of all relationships both in the office and in our private lives as well? All relationships are a work-in-progress and sometimes it is really tough but the benefits of doing those things necessary to make them better and more successful are immeasurable. Good quality relationships are the essence of a life of significance, good relationships with those with whom we work, with our friends, our family and also, our Creator.

Chapter IV
The Patient/Client

Would you like your patients to develop an even greater trust in you? Your staff will help you to do this if and when they are certain that you are trustworthy.

How do you view your patients? If they're simply a means to your financial gain you will have a hard time developing a long-term relationship with them and it will be difficult to achieve and enjoy the type of dentistry that most of us want.

If patients are to accept the very best treatment plan they must believe in and trust you. And that begins with their first phone call to your office. All of our patients enter our practice with a two hour new patient examination. During the first phone contact, the practice coordinator acquires the basic information from the patients:

1.   Patient's name and address

2.   Patient's phone number

3.   Who referred them to our office

4.   Their primary concerns and reason for calling

If they have an emergency we see them immediately. Otherwise they are scheduled for a new patient exam. The practice coordinator explains that we will do a thorough exam, take x-rays and initiate records and that the doctor will spend time to talk with them and address their concerns.

During the first appointment I introduce myself and talk with the patient and listen carefully to their concerns and I write them in the record. *Identifying their concerns is the most important part of the new patient exam–not diagnosing pathology.* If you fail to address their concerns during the new patient exam, you may never have the opportunity to address the pathology. *At this time, you must get past the patient's defenses and learn the real reason they are in a dental office and specifically why they are in your office.* We usually assume they only want us to fix their teeth, but this may be a mistake. You will need to ask the right questions in order to draw them out. ***Then listen … listen …***

> ***Hear*** *what they are really saying,* what they *really mean* and what they *really want from you. You need to talk about them–not about you.*

When you understand what they want, your job becomes much easier. They may not know exactly what they need or want, but when they know you're genuinely concerned about them, their trust level rises and they will be more inclined to believe you when you tell them what it's going to take to get them to a good state of dental health–whether it costs $350 or $35,000. You do not want to talk about what the treatment will cost at this point unless they ask about the cost of a specific procedure. Resist giving them an estimate of cost at this point or you will lose them. They will not hear you because they are thinking about the cost.

Questions I ask are included beginning on p. 97

As I begin the oral examination I preface the exam by a statement similar to one I learned from Dr. Bill Dickerson, the founder of The Las Vegas Institute of Advanced Dental Studies.

"If it's OK with you, I will record any defects I see. I will give you options to solve these problems and the costs of those options then you can decide if you want to accept my treatment recommendations or not.

Is that OK with you?"

Invariably the patient is very pleased because I have allowed them to remain in control. And in truth, they're in control anyway. By being very open and honest the patient doesn't feel like you are trying to sell them something and their "bologna detectors" don't go off. When we're honest and truthful, the patient senses/recognizes it and trust is being established.

The trust that the patient has in you is a very big responsibility because the patient will believe you and accept your recommendations for treatment. *This is not a manipulative ploy!* Honesty and trust are necessary for long term success and for developing a relationship that allows you to get them to a good state of dental health and maintain it as well as refer new patients to your practice.

New Patient Examination

As I do my clinical exam, my assistant guides me through a check list of questions. She will say, "Oral cancer exam." I explain everything as I am doing it. I will say that I am examining them for any lumps, lesions or any other abnormalities and I verbalize my findings so the assistant can note it in the record. I explain that I will do an examination of the teeth, gums, bone conditions and their bite–not occlusion, because I want and try to state everything in terms the patient can understand so that the patient will be involved in the process.

As I proceed through the clinical exam, I tell the assistant what I see so the patient can hear my findings. For example, I will say, "Number 14 upper-left molar has a broken filling and needs a crown." This way the patient has a mental picture of what I am seeing. When I begin the perio part of the exam, I explain that we are recording six measurements on each tooth. I explain what it means to their dental health and I tell them that I will do this again at future cleaning appointments so that I can monitor any changes. When I do the occlusal exam I explain any abnormalities I find especially if they have mentioned symptoms of any TMJ problems during the patient interview. At this time it is necessary to connect the cause of these symptoms with how they are caused by a malocclusion, since it is important for them to understand how the muscles and joints are affected by their teeth.

> *If you do not have a good understanding of how the system works, I would recommend postgraduate training at the Las Vegas Institute of Advanced Dental Studies or at Pete Dawson's seminar in Florida. I will write more about occlusion in a future book for it is also one of the secrets of success.*

At the conclusion of the new patient exam I do not give them my treatment recommendations unless it is very simple treatment. It is not until after I've had a chance to study the patient's x-rays and their models along with all the data I have collected. The patient is scheduled for a treatment conference appointment and it is then I explain the following:

1. *What* treatment I recommend

2. *Why* they need it

3. *What* they can expect from treatment

4. *How* much it will cost

At the end of the exam appointment ask if they have any questions; they always answer, "No, you made it clear."

Treatment Conference

At the treatment conference appointment I give them treatment options to fit within their budget and conform to their desires. This lets the patient know that they are still in control; they always appreciate that. The patient must always know they are in control and that they are able to make the decision as to whether or not they want to go forward with your recommendations. Allowing the patient to be in control is a major factor to earning their trust and their acceptance of proper and good treatment. During the treatment conference I reiterate that I am going to explain what their problems are, what treatment they need to correct them, and what it costs. I use an outline[4] to explain each step in an organized manner. First, the problem areas are identified and the solutions for each are explained. You want to make sure *that the patient "owns" their problems* and understands your recommendations. They will not accept treatment unless they acknowledge and own their problems.

Do not tell them how you will actually do a filling or a crown—they do not want to know technique!

Having already learned what their concerns are and how they feel about the appearance of their teeth during the new patient intake interview, I now ask if they have any questions. Many people do not like their smile. If the patient has mentioned any dissatisfaction with their smile, now is the time to offer your recommendations on how to improve their cosmetic appearance and get them to a place where they can feel good about their smile. In this era when people are living longer, their teeth age along with the rest of their body. People are spending big bucks on plastic surgery because they want to look better and people have the right to alter and improve their appearance if it is their desire.

After answering all their questions and learning what areas they are interested in, I tell them what the treatment will cost. When I'm sure they understand my recommendations, the practice coordinator enters to explain their payment options. After a clear understanding of how they will pay for treatment, she makes their first treatment appointment. This isn't done in the dental operatory because it is too threatening and uncomfortable. Being fair, honest and up front with their financial arrangements will also help them develop respect and trust in you. This does not mean your fees should be low. Quite the contrary! To provide above-average, high quality care you must charge a fee that is also higher than average.

In order to have patients who will refer others to you, you will have to give them better service than they expect to receive. This includes always being on time! Don't schedule a patient every half-hour or even hourly. Charge a fee that will allow you to spend adequate time with the patient. Dr. Omer Reed said that *all we have to offer is our care, skill and judgment.* And to those I would add, *our time.* If your schedule is rushed the patient will certainly know it and feel uncomfortable with your service. If you're running behind schedule all day, you are going to be tired and frazzled at the end of the day and that's no fun and that hectic schedule will lead to burn out. Design a schedule that allows you to begin on time, have lunch on time and finish the day on time. Am I always on time? No. But 95% of the time I am. And when I'm not, I apologize to the patient for making them wait and sometimes give them movie tickets or a gift card for lunch at a nice local restaurant.

Another rule to follow: *don't hurt the patient.* With modern dentistry almost everything can now be done without hurting the patient. Fear is the greatest hindrance to the patient following through with needed treatment. If you can't give a painless injection then learn a better technique. Fear of the needle may be the patient's greatest fear. Never let the patient even see the needle and be very caring when giving the injection. Years ago I heard a speaker say, "No one wants a jerk to stick a needle in their jaw." This is so true. If I inadvertently hurt someone I immediately apologized to them. Many of my patients comment on how easy the injection was. Painless injection technique is a real practice builder! And always make sure the anesthesia is fully effective before you proceed with the planned treatment.

Don't hesitate to let your patients know that you care about them. In the evening after the treatment, call and check on them. At the end of the day my assistant gives me a copy of the day's schedule with patient's phone number and the name of their spouse so that I can call on my way home from work. You will want to have their spouse's name in case they answer the phone. Patients are always impressed and grateful that I called. They always thank me and say that no other dentist or physician had ever done that for them. They rarely have any problems, but this one small act of kindness builds rapport and trust. Your cell phone has now become a business expense.

Another confidence and trust builder is the relationship they observe between you and your staff. Patients are keenly aware of how you treat your staff and how your staff responds to you. They are much more comfortable when the atmosphere in the office is warm and light during the procedures. I try to keep the mood in the operatory very upbeat and not stiff or uncomfortable. Patients want warmth with a gentle, caring spirit. My staff and I have a relationship that makes this possible as we can make little jokes or comments at appropriate moments and patients frequently hear me complimenting my staff when it was deserved. Many patients say that the entire experience was much better than they ever believed possible. This is how the experience in the operatory should and can be. If you haven't experienced this yet or are experiencing it infrequently, let me encourage you—you can!

The Operatory: Sterilization is a major concern for patients today and it's very obvious in our office that it is a concern of ours as well. Our rooms are much cleaner than rooms in many hospitals. When I enter the room I always wash my hands and make small talk to break the ice before entering the patient's "space". I explain the procedures planned for the day and answer any questions they might have. Every time I leave and reenter the room I wash my hands and patients often ask how many times a day I wash my hands. Of course I put on a new pair of gloves each time so many ask how many pairs of gloves I go through each day. The operatory is treated like a zone of high sterilization in a hospital. All the instruments are in their sterile packets and they can see that the fixed equipment and chair are covered in plastic. We explain that the plastic is replaced after each patient when the assistant sterilizes the room. The patient knows that we are giving them maximum protection; all of these steps relate to and builds trust and contributes to a successful practice. Most likely you also protect your patients in this way, so make them aware of it and they will have more confidence in you.

Entering the patient's space, as I sit down beside the patient I explain what I going to do so they will know what to expect. Before I position them for the procedure, I always touch the patient's shoulder and tell them I am going to lean the chair back. This is another preparatory step before invading their space. The mouth is a very personal space and we must be very gentle when approaching and invading "their privacy". Before beginning, I tell them I will be gentle and will make sure they are completely numbed before I begin and that if they hurt at anytime to be sure and let me know so I can take care of them. Throughout the procedure my assistant and I repeatedly ask if they are okay and not feeling any pain. They are very appreciative of that and by showing our concern they are more understanding and tolerant during an uncomfortable procedure. That old saying that *patients don't care how much you know until they know how much you care* is absolutely true. We must *earn* their trust. And when we do, we have relationships that last.

Avoid confusion: In the operatory I have a definite plan for the scheduled procedures. Each morning we have a team huddle and go over all scheduled treatment for each patient. When you do this, each member of the staff knows what to expect. The assistants are able to have all the required equipment and materials in place for every procedure making everything go more smoothly and efficiently. During the morning huddle, we bring up any special needs or concerns each patient may have. For example, if the patient recently had a tragedy in their life or a birthday coming up or if they're going on a trip, etc., *I am made* aware of it so that *I can* approach and respond to the patient appropriately. This concern or celebration with the patient is not artificial! It's no different than you would treat anyone you care about. It is you showing real concern for them and it makes a significant impact on the patient. Your patients want and need to know that they are important–not just a person with a number. Jim and Naomi Rhode also suggested the following and it has stayed with me through the years:

> *Imagine that each patient is sitting there with a large sign around their neck that says: "Make Me Feel Important!"* [5]

When you let the patient know that you have a plan just for them they will cut you some slack when something doesn't go exactly as you planned. Because fear and mistrust come from the unknown, make them feel comfortable by explaining everything you're doing. Your explanation should be generalized, not in specific terms of technique.

You know the words to avoid:

1. *"Oh no"*

2. *"Needle"*

3. *"Drill"*

4. *"Cut"*

You get the idea. Imagine yourself in their place and how you would want things explained to you if you didn't understand. It's just like they taught us in dental school–don't use invasive or harsh dental terms, rather keep them informed as the procedure progresses by explaining things in kind, simple terms. This will go a long way in calming their fears of the unknown.

Our patients are our most important referral base and as such should be highly valued and respected. Treat them like you would like to be treated.

Our philosophy statement is not simply some lofty words on a piece of paper. Each day, in interacting with each other and our patients we exemplify this philosophy.

Washing my hands when the treatment's completed, I thank them for allowing me to take care of them and let them know that I would be happy to take care of anyone they would like to refer to my office. This simple statement is a great for marketing.

When they refer a new patient to our office, I send a personal thank you note and a coffee mug with our logo. Patients always appreciate it when you take the time to let them know that they are important to you. This is an idea I learned from Dr. Rick Kushner of Table Mountain Seminars and this may be the best marketing technique I have ever used.

Sometimes at the end of the treatment, I give

the patient a "referral business card" which will earn them $50.00 on their on their next office visit after they have referred one of their friends to our office. This card also gives their friend a 2 hour new patient exam with x-rays and models free. It's a win-win-win deal for the referring patient, the new patient, and our office.

CHAPTER V
The Dentist

Self-assessment is not always fun. There are areas in which I continue to need improvement. The areas of my life and practice that I would offer to be of high importance to give us success are 1) attitude 2) interest in continuing education 3) the level of pride we take in our work and 4) proper time management. I propose that we are all a work-in-progress and that for me, I continue to need help.

As dentists, we are on a journey in our ever changing dental practice, and as it morphs, we are enjoying it sometimes more–sometimes less. The enjoyable times are usually when we have a great staff, the right patients, and money left over at the end of the month. To help you have more of those times and enjoy your journey, allow me to suggest that you take a real *honest* and very *personal* look within yourself. Read that last sentence again; it may be the most important one in the book. Honest self-evaluation is essential in our personal life and professional development.

Attitude
Our attitude may be the determinant in whether we will enjoy happiness or unhappiness, success or failure. How we view life each morning depends to a large degree on how we have answered life's deepest questions concerning our origin and purpose and destiny.

Where did we come from? Why are we here... and where are we going? Since I believe there is a divine calling for each one of us, I believe that we can receive divine inspiration as motivation to do what we do and with that we can derive satisfaction in life but we have to answer the divine call. Please don't think I'm bragging– I'm just another human being like you. But I have come to terms with life's deeper questions that will confront each one of us at some point before we die.

I am happy with the work that my Creator has given me and this in turn gives me a positive attitude and that is something that everyone needs if they are to get things done and enjoy life. Do I always have a great attitude? No. And my wife, Laverne and my patients and staff will tell you so. But the bad attitude days are few because I have hope–the hope that the Creator gives us shines through even on gloomy days. It is a hope that anyone can have by just asking the Creator God for it.

Continuing Education
Continuing Education keeps dentistry fun and challenging! Dentistry is constantly changing at such a pace that I cannot keep up with all of it. However, being exposed to new ideas, techniques and dynamic teaching is really energizing and associating with other students in our profession in their quest for professional knowledge and skill is truly fun. Attending high quality meetings is necessary if we are to avoid burn out. I come away from all the meetings with a couple of pearls. But as with everything in life–you get what you pay for, even in dental education. The courses from which I reap the most benefits are the ones that last more than

a day and involve hands-on patient treatment and cost the big bucks. I've listened to a multitude of practice management people; some were good and some were a disaster. Don't take everything you hear from a speaker as gospel; evaluate it very carefully before you implement it. On the other hand, many dentists attend seminars and never change a thing in their practice and that too is a huge mistake unless you want your practice to be the same year in and year out. What a rut! Besides being boring, that limits the potential growth of your practice.

Yes, those seminars that involve multiple days and treating patients cost more and we must close the office, but in these meetings we learn and experience dynamic change and growth. For a big boost in growth and motivation take your entire staff with you! It will raise their skill level. It will set them on fire! So turn them loose and watch things happen!

Decide the types of treatment you enjoy the most and become proficient in them. We cannot be an expert in everything. Decide what you want to become an expert in and become that expert by availing yourself to the best teaching available. When we know that we are good at those things success is predictable and dentistry becomes a lot more fun.

My post-graduate work has mostly been in cosmetics and occlusion because I enjoy these aspects of dentistry and have had good success in those areas. It is when we enjoy our work and experience positive results that we actually have fun, avoid burnout and make money.

Take Pride in Your Work

Another important key to having and enjoying success is to decide to take pride in everything you do. This was instilled in us at University of Tennessee School of Dentistry. This is not egotism. I want to be the very best dentist I can be and never be ashamed of anything that comes out of my office. I want to create restorations that I would be willing to put my initials on like we did in dental school. Am I proud of everything I have done? Absolutely not! But I've always done the best I could do under the conditions and circumstances of any particular day. I have learned not to criticize my peers whenever I see a crown that would not meet clinical standards because also I too may not have done as well under the conditions that were presented to him or her on that particular day he or she did the work.

A motivation that influences me to take pride in the dentistry I do is the fact that I am in a group practice. Let me explain. Currently at Cornerstone[6] I have four partners. We all have separate practices but share facilities, equipment, and some staff members. The following doctors and I were the founders of this group: Dr. Dan Anderson who is still a partner; Dr. Fred Woolwine who has since relocated out of Knoxville, and Dr. Jim McKinney who is now a dental consultant. As a group, we established guidelines governing how we would practice together and relate to one another. It was a wonderful practicing relationship and those relationships continue even though two of them are gone and have been replaced by Dr. Mark Britton, Dr. Joe Griffin and Dr. Ben Stroud. All of these men are fantastic, successful dentists, fun guys who inspire me to be the best I can be. We are accountable to each other as our names are linked together and our community reputation will rise or fall together. There is a great synergism among us which motivates and comforts me, because I know that, if need be, they are there to pull the bacon out of the fire for me. Many group practices don't work out but ours has been solid for 21 wonderful years. *The main reason our partnership works is that we all share the same core values.* As two of the original partners retired or moved, we have taken on three new partners who are not only fantastic dentists, but who also share the same core values.

To associate with other practitioners in whom we can trust and from whom we can learn is very beneficial to success. If you are in a practice by yourself, develop a study club of colleagues and friends with whom you meet to help each other grow. Your group can share ideas, solve problems, study new techniques, inspire each other, bring in a teacher for a private seminar, attend seminars together or conduct a book study. The point is—"... iron sharpens iron" (Proverbs 20:17), *and we can inspire each other so that our work is more successful, more fun, rewarding and profitable.*

What we desire energizes and drives us.

If we:

Desire to be the best dentist we can be, we find a high level of success, enjoyment and profit.

If we:

Desire to be wealthy, the money is never enough and we will discover that life becomes a daily grind and we experience burnout.

This may seem a little simplistic, but the basic premise is true: if we are striving primarily for wealth we will never be fully satisfied and it will eventually lead to an unhappy practice-life. Conversely, when we are trying to be the best dentist we can be, we will experience a true sense of self-worth and a positive attitude and the patients and staff will know it and the practice grows and becomes better and more profitable.

With the right motivation we get it all; satisfaction in a job well-done and an increase in income.

Proper Time Management

I have to work hard in this area in my personal life. I am continually tempted to have too many projects going at the same time. Each hour of time is an opportunity that we have but once so we have to learn how to balance it between two extremes—doing nothing and trying to do too much. Either one will waste the time we have and in its own insidious way, prevent us from being successful. In the 21st Century, there are so many things available, each one competing for our time, and if we aren't careful, they can captivate our thoughts, drain our energy, devour our time, and cause us to fail to reach our goals. The Apostle Paul, writing to the Ephesians in about 60AD, said it all much more succinctly in Ephesians, Chapter 5:15–17:

Look carefully then how you walk, not as unwise but as wise, making the best use of the times because the days are evil.

Therefore do not be foolish, but understand what the will of the Lord is.

So truly, there is nothing new. Everyone has been tempted to waste time since the beginning of time itself. But today, there are so many more things to attract us and cause us to waste precious time and derail us from attaining our goals.

Setting goals is of utmost importance if we are to achieve our goals and realize our dreams. The most important step toward achieving our goals is to first *define* our goals and *write them down*. When we write them down they become more real to us. Next, *prioritize* the steps you will have to take to achieve those goals and *work on them one step at-a-time*. This system has worked well for me notwithstanding my poor time-management skills.

Some of the things that cause us to waste time and fail to reach our goals include:

1. Procrastination

2. Failure to prioritize tasks

3. Attempting too much at once

4. Setting unrealistic time estimates

5. Reluctance to get started

6. Lacking confidence

7. Fearing failure

You know that you have the intelligence and the staying power necessary to succeed. Your dreams are within your reach. I know this is true because of what you have already achieved in life. Only a very small percentage of people are accepted into dental school and not every one of them graduates. Most of you already have a good dental practice and want it to be even better. The fact that you are taking the time to read a book on how to improve your practice places you in the very small company of high-achievers. You are on your way! Begin now by prioritizing your dreams and goals. Organize your thoughts. Write them down and number them.

Dentists are very susceptible to certain pitfalls. You know the stats: dentists lead the universe in divorce, suicide, alcoholism and drug addiction. One piece of advice I would offer–*get out of debt!* Debt may be our biggest enemy in the quest to achieve our life goals. The stress of a debt burden causes us much grief. Debt has an insidious way of growing out of control and causes us to lose hope. And it is very difficult to function when we have no hope. The stress of debt can even kill you. But let me give you hope! Please listen and believe this from someone who has been in debt: You can get out of debt! Get started on your way to success–write down your goals even though you don't know how it is possible to reach them right now.

Chapter VI
Dental Economics 101

When I was in dental school our only practice management course taught us that if we wanted to make a million dollars a year we should: A) find a patient who was willing to pay us a million dollars to fix their teeth, B) find a two patients who would pay us $500,000 dollars each to fix their teeth, or C) find four patients who would pay us $250, 000 each—you get the picture. At the time I thought that was a pretty stupid class, but I have since come to appreciate what the professor was suggesting but never came right out and said; you could also see a million patients and charge them $1.00 each. Well that certainly doesn't fly well either. But the point is this—you must decide where *you* want to fit on that scale. Many dentists never make that decision and land on the fee scale by default. Most just go with the average fee structure and simply blend in with their neighborhood or they go low hoping to attract more patients.

Where you are on the fee scale of either high fees or low fees should be determined by your philosophy of dentistry. I reiterate: decide which market you want to serve and what types of dentistry you want to do. If you are inclined to serve the lower income market then obviously your fees would need to be below the national average and you will be forced to see enough patients and perform enough procedures to meet your overhead and make a profit, otherwise you will not be able to continue to serve them. Serving the lower income market is a noble and good thing to do. However, you will be limited in the type of dentistry you will do daily.

In service to this market, I personally choose to donate my services at an indigent clinic in the U.S. or abroad, or treat low-income patients in my office at reduced cost, or free of charge, depending on their needs and ability to pay.

If your fees are low you will be forced to see more patients and spend less time with each one. The danger here of course is that you won't be able to maintain high quality care in that type of situation because a tension exists between high quality care and a low fee structure.

In the late 70s, a group of six dentists, including myself, decided that many people could not afford dentures in our upscale offices and decided to open a denture clinic in Knoxville, Tennessee. Ethically, we decided that we could not extract any teeth and make the dentures because we did not want to simply create edentulous mouths just for us to fill up our schedules and pockets.

We decided to offer three levels of service: economy, standard, and best dentures. Since we used our best care, skill, and judgment to make each level of denture, we soon learned that all three levels of dentures delivered in our office were the same except for the quality of the materials used. We always did our best. We took the same amount of time and used the best techniques to make each denture. I had some great partners. And for a while, we had fun and made some money. During this time I was discovering which market I should be in.

In the same time period, Sears decided to put dental offices in their stores nationwide. They contacted me in Knoxville and offered me an opportunity to open dental offices in all their Tennessee locations. I would operate and manage clinics which would offer dental services at lower fees than what most of my peers or I charged in our private practices. In a retail environment I would need to advertise the low fees in order to attract Sears' customers. During this time I was experiencing back problems so severe that I thought it was going to force me out of wet fingered dentistry and as a result, I would not deliver the dentistry myself but enter into the field of dental management. The first thing I had to do was find dentists who would work in a fast-paced retail environment *and* deliver high quality care. I found some and we served people well. But there was no profit for me–the investor/owner. I made the mistake in believing that we could give people high quality care for low fees and make up for it with high volume. It was a very expensive lesson for me.

This experience motivated me to clarify and refine the principles in my head and heart in regard to the type of dentistry I wanted to devote my life to. I realized that I wanted to perform the highest quality dentistry of which I am capable, using the best techniques possible. To do that would necessitate: 1) continuing education, 2) extra time given to each patient, 3) state-of-the-art equipment, 4) the services of more costly dental labs and, 5) a higher fee structure to support it. I was now actively developing my philosophy of care for my future in dentistry.

My partners at Sears shared this philosophy so we built a state-of-the-art facility and moved out of the clinic environment to deliver dental care based upon that philosophy.

The education I received from the Sears experience was expensive but it focused my head and heart and led me to develop a new and lasting philosophy. I had to make a choice between low fees and a high volume of patients in basic dentistry or high fees and a lower volume of patients whom I would serve using advanced cutting edge techniques. You simply cannot be in both markets simultaneously and be highly successful. I enjoy seeing one patient per-day and giving that patient a beautiful, healthy smile and a completely rebuilt occlusion.

We are so fortunate to be practicing in this golden age of dentistry. Our population is living longer, but our body parts are wearing out—knees, hips *and teeth*. Modern medicine and dentistry have techniques to replace those things. Medical insurance pays for knees and hips but dental insurance will only pay for about one or two teeth per year. If we are to restore broken down occlusions, full mouth reconstruction cannot be done one tooth-at-a-time. Dental insurance will not cover the cost of restoring a smile. But Baby Boomers really want that beautiful smile and many have the money to support their desire. The point is this: dental insurance should not dictate the treatment that the patient needs, desires or receives. And we need to be proactive in educating patients to this fact! The yearly dental benefits the patient received in the 70s was about $1,000 per year, and the yearly benefits today is still about the same even though the cost of care has gone up from about $75 per crown to about $1,000 per crown today.

Don't let dental insurance plans dictate your fees!

If you join a dental insurance plan that will send

patients to you, then you have agreed to their low fee structure, the insurance company is controlling your practice. And that's okay if that is the market you want to be in. But please realize that you cannot switch back and forth between the two. You cannot serve a patient on the low fee scale and then switch gears for the next patient who has a high-quality, high-fee state-of-mind. Human nature will not allow us to switch gears that way. Many years ago the local dental lab I was using let their quality decline. I knew they were capable of high quality dentistry and had three meetings with the owners about the problem. They said they could not give my lab work more time and attention than they gave other dentists' cases. They had not increased their fees in some time and when I suggested that they charge me more and give my cases more time in order to achieve the quality that my practice and patients demanded, they said they couldn't do it and I was forced to change dental labs.

I now use two dental labs: one owned by Steve Clark who serves all my partners at Cornerstone Dental Arts and the other lab technician who does my work is Young Kim formerly of MICRODENTAL | a dti company [formerly MicroDental Laboratories of California]. Both of these labs are high quality labs and the fees they charge reflect it. The point is this: I cannot use a high quality lab and charge low fees. It will not work. Decide on the market you want to serve.

The low fee treadmill will burn you out and make life miserable. So how do you get off the dark treadmill of low fee dentistry and into the light of fun dentistry?

The First Step

1. *Get out of debt.* Make a commitment to get out of personal debt and learn to live on what you make. Set up a budget based on your average monthly income and live on it. You must also set aside your IRS payments first and budget the income that remains. This will require self-discipline. But I did it and so can you! So much of this is common sense and yet it's amazing the number of dentists who have to borrow money to pay their taxes and then pay interest on the tax money! DUMB! The lure of toys causes us to fall into that awful pit and the resulting stress will destroy a quality life, relationships and hope for achieving your dreams. Don't buy the toys until you can pay cash for them. Yes, that is possible.

A few years ago I read an incredible bestseller by authors Thomas J. Stanley and William D. Danko, *The Millionaire Next Door.* I recommend you read this book just to see how millionaires *think.* In the early 1990s I sat in on a great lecture at the Hindman Dental Meeting in Atlanta, Georgia. One of the speakers suggested that people who were interested in getting out of debt read *The Richest Man in Babylon.* I read it and it impacted my life. Long story short: *I am out of debt. I live in a big, beautiful, mortgage-free house on the lake and I sleep well at night.* I have the toys too: a boat, boat dock, pool and a beautiful white Corvette convertible which I love to drive. But when I heard that lecture I was so broke that I was borrowing money each month to live on. The investment I made in the Sears clinic had been very costly; I had very poor self-discipline in my personal life and I was not living on a budget. My wife and I went through some very hard times because of my lack of financial control and poor self-discipline.

I have made some bad decisions in my personal and financial life and also in my practice. But I turned it around and you can too. As I write this part of the book, my wife and I are in Cabo San Lucas, Mexico for a Frontier Dental Lab dental seminar. In the last fourteen months we have been on two, seven-day cruises and a trip to Europe. I'm not telling you these things to boast. I am telling you to encourage those of you who feel that you cannot achieve a successful dental practice and get out of debt.

The Second Step

2. *Don't be an employee of a dental insurance company.* Get off dental insurance plans that dictate your fees! Stop accepting the insurance benefits as your payment or partial payment. Don't place yourself between your patient and their insurance plan. Do not let the insurance company dictate your fees and thus affect your diagnosis and limit or determine what is best for your patients. Since 1987 my practice has been a fee-for-service practice which means my patients pay me on the day of service. I offer a 10% discount for cash payment and patients almost always choose that method of payment. I also offer to help them use a financial plan like Wells Fargo so they can stretch their payments over 12 months at no interest and there are many of those types of plans. They also have the option of using a credit card for which I give a 5% discount. By using these options my accounts

receivable usually runs $3 - 4,000 per month. Those of you who have high accounts receivable are loaning your patients your profit.

Dollars from production - dollars from collection = loans to patients at 0% interest.

Profit you may never get.

The Third Step

3. *Your fee structure should reflect quality care.* Increase your fees and give your patients your very best care, skill and judgment. In our area, my fee structure compares with those at the higher end bracket. There are four other dentists in the same building who operate the same way and all of them are successful. We are a group in the same facility but all have separate practices. High-quality care must be supported by an appropriate fee structure.

The Fourth Step

4. *Increase your knowledge and skill by attending high-quality continuing education.* You and your staff need to attend high quality continuing education seminars. This will improve the quality of services you provide to your patients. Yes—it's expensive. But it will not only raise the standard of your services but also change your mind set. You will begin to think differently and approach your patients differently. There are many quality advanced training programs you can attend. For example:

- The Pankey Institute

- The American Academy of Cosmetic Dentistry Seminars.

- The Las Vegas Institute for Advanced Dental Studies;

- Frontier Dental Lab Seminars;

- MICRODENTAL | a dti company Seminars;

There other seminars conducted by individuals such as

- Dr. Nate Booth;

- Dr. Duke Heller in Ohio;

- Dr. Larry Rosenthal in New York and

- Dr. Pete Dawson in Florida.

I've attended most of these but there are many others from which to choose. These seminars are not simply two or three hour lectures, and many include hands-on instruction treating patients. They are expensive. But they will literally change your life. If you want to get off the treadmill of dentistry, attending high-quality seminars is a worthwhile investment.

Take your staff with you so they too can catch the vision and join you in your journey to success. When you return to the office, schedule an all-day staff meeting and change things! Too many dentists go to meetings only to satisfy their required credits but they return to their practices and never change anything. Implement changes in your practice!

Chapter VII
Practice Transitions, from Early Years to Selling the Practice

In my first year of practice I contracted Professional Budget Plan[7] to coach me. They came to my office, observed the practice dynamics of a typical workday and recommended changes. They saved me a lot of grief and money by setting up bookkeeping and accounting systems and teaching me valuable internal marketing methods. They taught me the techniques of an effective case presentation that I'm still using today. This set the course that led me on my way to success. I highly recommend that you consider someone from outside your practice to come in and identify, and evaluate your present system and make recommendations that will help you succeed. When I contracted Professional Budget Plan to help me, I was so poor that I thought I could not afford it. I was wrong. This was something that I could not afford not to do. You have heard this pitch many times, but in this case … it was true, and may be true for you also.

When I graduated from dental school I hadn't been taught anything about how to run a business, manage a practice or a staff. The secret is to quickly get quality help. And it will cost you some bucks. But coaching may be what you need to help you on your journey to success. We all have to think properly about our business and then manage it. We need the tools (systems) just like we had to invest in dental tools (instruments).

Thankfully, I had some help over the years. My practice transitioned from early growth to struggling, to highly successful and profitable, working only eleven days per month.

Since beginning this book in 2003, four years have passed and I want to share the changes that have taken place in my practice.

Mrs. Sue Marshall[8], a dental team coach, of Dental Boot Kamp, called me out of the blue one day and said there was a great student at the University of Tennessee Memphis Medical Units, Mark Britton, who was scheduled to graduate and that I should talk to him about becoming an associate. I explained that things were going great and that I was not looking for an associate but she continued to insist that I meet him. Since Sue and I had enjoyed a good, long-term relationship, I agreed to meet him.

He and I scheduled a short, "get acquainted" meeting, and after a two hour visit, both Dr. Britton and I knew that he was supposed to be at Cornerstone Dental Arts. We scheduled another meeting, and after talking for four hours it was basically a done deal. We agreed to these basic principles; I would bring him into my practice as an associate for a three month period, and if all went well, he would buy my practice and I would become his employee. All went well. Now when there is a problem, I can say "Ain't my job … I just work here." This has been a win-win-win. Dr. Mark Britton is a blessing to all of us at Cornerstone Dental Arts. He is an excellent dentist. The staff and I enjoy his high quality standards, his caring spirit and his very quick wit.

At first, the staff was very skeptical and guarded about the practice transition to Dr. Britton. During the transition period, the staff *must* be considered because *they hold the keys to an easy and successful transition.* The patients will look to and depend upon the staff for validation of the new doctor! When the staff is on the same page as both the buyer and the seller you have a success story.

My Staff

I have often referred to my staff at Cornerstone Dental Arts, all of whom have been major players in my success story.

I would like to tell you a little about the lovely, wonderful women on our team, all of whom I respect, value and sincerely like. Allow me to introduce them:

Mary Anne King is our hostess at Cornerstone Dental Arts. She greets all the patients as they arrive and signals the appropriate team. She is a sweet, lovely lady. Her responsibility is to make the new arrivals comfortable and welcomed. She serves coffee, tea, hot chocolate, and cookies.

Amy Vittetoe is our newest staff member. She was one of the best in her dental assistant graduating class. Not only are her skills excellent–she has a gentle approach and wonderful attitude which the patients appreciate and love. Some people are fun to be around, and this is Amy.

Shannon Hays is a fantastic dental hygienist who now works part-time, but she does much more than clean teeth. She has been the "get 'er done girl" on my team for fourteen years. All I had to do was *think* of implementing something in the practice and she made it happen. Every dental practice needs 'energizing bunnies', and she is pure joy.

Pam Krieger (or Poo as I call her), is our great practice coordinator who returned to our practice after a period of time away from us. She is a joy to work with. We have worked together for nearly nine years and she lifts my spirits each time I pass her desk. She is always there to encourage me during a difficult day when I need a 'pick-me-up'.

Sonya Todd is my faithful right hand assistant of eighteen years. I am thankful for her talents and truly enjoy working with her. She makes the difficult cases much easier and permits me to keep the atmosphere in the operatory light by kidding her. She kids me too! In case you don't know, anything that goes wrong in the operatory is always the fault of the assistant. The fault can never lie with the patient; they are the guest of honor. The fault can never lie with the doctor; after all The Doctor and everyone else knows that Doctors don't make mistakes. Therefore since the assistant is the only one left she is at fault and must accept the blame. Somehow I haven't been able to get either Sonya or Amy to buy into it. And on occasion I blame it on the lab. The point is this: Sonya allows me to use humor (often at her expense) to keep a light air during some of the more difficult or tedious treatment procedures.

Gwen Lange is our super hygienist of eleven years. She is a fantastic hygienist and a patient magnet. Area practices have lost patients because those patients were looking for her—not me. One of my best friends, who is also a patient, told me that if Gwen ever leaves, he's going to follow her. Both Gwen and Shannon have very skillful, gentle hands and our patients love them.[9] Gwennie (as I call her) is an elegant, gracious lady who brings her solid core-values with her every day.

Lori Johnson (or Sunshine as I call her) is the office

facilitator behind the scene. Her responsibilities lie with the computer and accounting systems. Both she and Mary Anne serve all of us at Cornerstone, not just the team of Dr. Britton and me. Sunshine has been the brains behind Cornerstone for over 20 years.

At the beginning of each week I announce a meeting of these lovely ladies that a new contest is starting to see who gets to be my favorite for the week. Somehow, I can never get them really involved since they don't see the value of just being my favorite. I tell this inside joke I have with the women and I share it only as an illustration of the light air that can exist when everyone is pulling together. Each of these women is a unique, highly motivated individual; all of the intangible qualities they bring are needed to make up that great team.

You may think it's impossible to find really great staff members but let me encourage and assure you that it can be done and it's worth the effort. At Cornerstone, we have a staff of twenty-four great professionals and each one of them is dependable, honest and fun to work with. Each dentist thinks his staff is the best–and that's as it should be. You can find, hire and retain a fantastic team player if you treat them well.

An uncomplicated, successful transition of a practice from one doctor to another is largely dependent upon the staff, but there are some other important things that help to make a transition easier. First, you must have the terms of agreement in writing! This sounds so elementary yet so many times there is nothing in writing. Failure to put the details in writing can lead to a lot of misunderstandings and often results in broken relationships and bank accounts. I've heard the horror stories and most of the time it was the selling doctor who left himself/herself vulnerable and got burned.

Never Break This Rule: *Always have a written agreement.* I don't care who it is. Even if it is your best friend or son or daughter; those relationships are even more vulnerable. Have a letter of understanding that places the potential buyer as an independent contractor with the practice with an option to purchase the practice. After three months, any one of three things could happen:

> The buyer buys out the seller and the seller becomes the associate. Now the seller has the responsibility to help the patients accept the new doctor. This gives more value to the practice to prevent loss of patients.

> Either the buyer or seller decides that the three-month trial period should continue (that is the buyer continues as the associate for an agreed upon time).

> Either party decides that this relationship cannot work and either party can end the relationship. The potential buyer agrees that he/she will not practice within ten miles of the seller's office.

The letter of understanding should include the following:

- The monetary compensation for the associates, whether buyer or seller

- The work schedules for both buyer and seller

- New buyer or associate's proof of valid license

- The stated purpose of the agreement which is to get to know each other and decide if either or both parties want to move forward

- The stated value of the practice at the time of the agreement signing and the amount the buyer is to pay the seller upon closing the sale of the practice

The buyer and seller must meet with an attorney or attorneys to have these things drawn up:

1. A letter of understanding or intent to buy.

2. A buy/sell contract.

3. An outline of the responsibilities of both parties during the transition phase (or the roles each doctor will play as the selling doctor's responsibilities decrease).

4. An agreement stating that until the day the contract to sell is signed, either party can change their mind and rescind their offer.

Important things that make a practice more attractive to the buyer:

1. The practice should be showing signs of growth

2. There should be a healthy profit margin

3. An attractive facility; it's like buying a house–curb appeal is important

4. Good equipment, updated and in good working order

5. Committed great staff–Tired of hearing me talk about a great staff? You get the idea of how valuable they are. They are essential for a smooth transition.

Practicing with Dr. Britton is a blessing for me and has been great fun for the dentists and staff at Cornerstone Dental Arts. Bringing him on board has been great. But as in all relationships, there were bumps along the way. That's the way life is. But if everyone is open, honest and sincerely wants to make it work and is willing to give and take, it can be negotiated.

Because Dr. Britton and I can help each other and we enjoy our working relationship, I continue to work at Cornerstone two days per week.

I am very thankful and feel very blessed to continue to practice with Dr. Britton and the entire staff at Cornerstone.

Chapter VIII
The Bottom Line

I continue to work about eight days a month because it is still fun. Laverne and I enjoy living here in Knoxville, Tennessee. We enjoy our home and love to travel. We have a large family, three married children and eight beautiful grandchildren. For me, that is success in life and in dentistry.

How do we define success? Many people equate success with making a lot of money and living the "good life" filled with glitz and toys. However, both you and I can think of the names of many jet-set people who seemed to have it all but whose lives ended in tragedy.

I would offer this as success: *When we come to the end of our life and stand before the grave and can look back at our lives and be pleased with what we see.*

The view would include:

1. Feeling content with what you've accomplished in life and the legacy you leave.

2. Having developed quality relationships with family and friends.

3. Having served our patients and employees with integrity, high quality care and compassion.

I have not arrived nor have I achieved it all, but those are the things that have lasting value and substance. I am still trying to be the best dentist I can be, the best husband I can be, the best father and grandfather I can be and the best friend I can be to my friends.

The bottom line of success comes down to our core values, those things that drive us to get out of bed each morning. The French philosopher, scientist and mathematician Blaise Pascal said that everyone has a God-shaped vacuum in their heart that must be filled with something. We can fill it with self, but that will only lead to discontentment and emptiness. However, if we fill it with God, He promises to give us a life of fulfillment. Is that a rose garden filled with bliss? No. But it is a life of contentment and it works for me.

In this book I have tried to give you some direction in how to have success in your dental practice. But the success story must initially begin with exploring and addressing some of life's deepest questions. For me, I believe we all must first answer this fundamental question: "What is my purpose on this earth?" I am not saying to be successful one must be a Christian, but I believe we all must discover our life's purpose on earth if life is to have real meaning. If there is no God or Divine Creator, then hedonism is the way to go and just enjoy life the best you can. However, if there is a God who gave you life then the key to success is to get *to know Him and discover the plan He has for you.*

The bottom line summary of my thoughts on the pathway to success is:

1. Discover your purpose on this earth. Ask God the Creator to reveal Himself and His purpose for you.

2. Nurture relationships; people are what is important.

3. Improve yourself in what you do and become the best you can be.

4. Don't let the love of money rule and ruin your life.

Scripture says in I Timothy 6:10 that the love of money is the root of all evil and causes a lot of grief (paraphrased). Notice that money itself in *not* the problem; the problem lies in the *love* of money.

What will all this mean to us five-hundred years from now? Well, if *I've* been wrong about God giving us meaning in life there are no consequences for me and that pursuit of God has led me through life to success and contentment on this earth. If the *atheist* is wrong and there is a Creator God to whom we must answer, then for him or her, the consequences are *eternal.*

I have shared aspects of my faith with you and I respect your right to your own personal beliefs which may be very different from mine. I hope and pray that you are able to apply and benefit from some of the ideas I've shared with you as you travel on life's journey and as well as in your dental practice venture.

May the Lord I serve bless you is my prayer for all those who read these words.

EPILOGUE

The following is a chronicle of the part of my journey that lead me to the place where I found peace and meaning to my life.

Growing up in many parts of our great nation, Mom and Dad took me to church and gave me a proper upbringing as the Greatest Generation often did for their children. I then went to college and was exposed to the greatest thinkers and philosophers our world has produced. Even though I went to a Presbyterian college, because of the radical ideas of my professors, I came out of college as an agnostic with communist/socialist leanings, and these ideas continue to be prevalent and are promulgated among the leaders of academia today.

For the most part, in college my religion was put on the shelf and I lived the fraternity party life that continued through dental school and through my days spent in the United States Navy. But even then God was dealing with me in those wild years. There were Sunday mornings I found myself in churches of different denominations because God was drawing me to seek the truth. I had that God-shaped vacuum in my heart that had to be filled. While in the Navy, stationed in Chicago, I went to a bookstore and bought a Bible but hid it from my friends because I was embarrassed. I read it in secret but did not understand the main thing of the Scripture.

After the Navy, I moved to Knoxville, Tennessee, where I met and married my beautiful wife, Laverne.

I thought she would fill that hole in my soul. But as lovely as she is she could not take the place that God wanted in my life. We became leaders in a Christian church where we were married and also took our children every Sunday. While sitting in church one Sunday, I asked myself *"Is this real? Is Jesus who He said He is; did He really arise from the dead and is He God? Or even is there really a God or not?"* I decided to seriously seek the truth. If Christ is who He said He is then I really needed to get with the program. But if He was only the figment of someone's imagination I did not need a Sunday morning country club. Someone said that when the student is ready the teacher will arrive and God sent Ken Neff, a new graduate of Dallas Theological Seminary. Ken explained the basic essentials of Christianity that I had failed to grasp.

God, the Architect and Creator of heaven and earth, sent His Son Jesus to live on this earth and suffer for our sins. He lived a sinless life and died on a cross outside of Jerusalem in about 30 AD. On the third day, He arose from the dead to reveal to everyone who care to believe and follow Him that He can give them eternal life. Jesus said in John 10:10, *"I came that they might have life and have life more abundantly."*

Ken explained that if I decided that I wanted to become a Christian that I should ask Christ to forgive me of my sin and come into my life—not just become a member of a church. I already had my name on a church membership list but I was not a disciple of Jesus. The steps that I took are clearly presented in the Bible:

I must confess that I am a sinner and in need of a Savior. Romans 3:23–24

Jesus Christ is God and loves everyone and offers everyone eternal life if they believe in Him. John 3:16

Ask Jesus to come into our life (receive Him) and then we become a Christian–a child of the Living God. John 1:12

Ken Neff explained these things to me and I pondered them in my heart for a couple of days. Driving home by myself after work one rainy afternoon, I decided to take those steps in prayer. I was on the Interstate 40/75 and started praying as I approached the Cedar Bluff exit and by the time I reached the end of the exit, I had made that commitment and God gave me eternal life. My life changed dramatically and I knew what it meant to be a Christian. He filled that hole in my soul and I found the peace that I had been seeking. That was about thirty-seven years ago and Christ has *NEVER* let me down even through the hard times.

When we make that commitment to Christ, He makes us a promise in I John 5:13: We can then know for sure [not simply hope] that we have an eternal life. That promise excludes no one. It's available to everyone. It is not exclusive. It was my choice. It is your choice. And it's the best deal I have ever made!

Medical History

Patient Name

Have you ever had?

Rheumatic Fever	Yes	No
Heart Problems	Yes	No
Hepatitis	Yes	No
High or Low Blood Pressure	Yes	No
Tuberculosis	Yes	No
Anemia	Yes	No
Diabetes	Yes	No
Asthma	Yes	No
Allergies	Yes	No
X-Ray Treatment for Tumor or Growth	Yes	No
Fainting Spells or Seizures	Yes	No

Any Others?

Are you allergic to **ANY** drugs or medicines such as penicillin, codeine or aspirin?

Yes   No

If so, what?

Are you taking drugs now?   Yes   No

If so, what?

Do you bleed for a long time when you get a cut?

Yes   No

Have you had a medical examination within the last year?

Yes   No

Have you been hospitalized or had a serious illness within the past 5 years?

                                            Yes   No

If so, what for?

Are you under a physician's care now?   Yes   No

If so, why?

Names of Physicians

OFFICE GUIDE
FIRST APPOINTMENT and NEW PATIENT EXAMINATION

Initial Interview

- •Explain the new patient exam.
- •Most important thing that will happen today is for you to tell me about yourself.
- •I treat people the way I want to be treated.

1. I do not want to hurt when I have my teeth fixed.

2. With your permission, I will recommend treatment for any unhealthy teeth the way I would want it fixed in my mouth with the finest dentistry available.

3. It will be your job to decide if you want to do that and in what time frame.

4. How does that sound to you?

Dental History

- •How can we help you?
- •Do you have any dental problems or sensitive teeth?

1. Do your gums bleed when you brush?

2. Have you ever had gum (periodontal) treatment?

3. Do you have any sores or lumps in your mouth?

4. Do you have trouble chewing your food?

5. How long has it been since your last dental exam?

6. When was your last cleaning?   scheduled yes or no

7. Your last dental x-rays?

8. How often do you get your teeth cleaned?

9. How long do you expect to keep your teeth?

10. Why did you leave your previous dentist?

11. What did you like about your previous dentist?

12. Do you smoke?

13. Do you feel that you suffer from bad breath?

Smile Analysis

1. On a scale of 1–10 how would you rate your teeth when you smile?

2. If you could wave a magic wand what would you change about your teeth?

3. Would you like to see how you would look if your smile was improved? Smile? Lift?

4. Would you like to have whiter teeth?

TMJ Screen

1. History of TMJ problems?

2. Joint soreness or tenderness with function?

3. History of jaw injury?

4. Joint sounds? When?

5. Headaches? N/A

6. Jaws lock or go out of joint?

7. Do you clinch or grind your teeth?

What is most important to you when you need dental services?

Dr. William R. Morgan

SECOND APPOINTMENT
Case Presentation / Treatment Conference

Patient Concerns

II. Patient Current Condition

A) Foundation (Periodontal)

B) Teeth

   1.   Missing

   2.   Decayed or broken

C. Occlusion

   1.   TMJ Condition

   2.   Occlusal Problems

D. Cosmetic Issues

   1.   Alignment

   2.   Spacing

   3.   Color

   4.   Other

III. Treatment

A) Foundation

1. Prophylaxis
2. STM
3. Home Care

B) Teeth

1. Remove _____

2. Restore _____

    a. Composite Resin _____

    b. Onlay/Crown/Veneers _____

    c. Fixed Bridges _____

    d. Removal - Partial Dentures

C) Occlusion

1. Orthotic Splint Therapy
2. Equilibration
3. Reconstruction

D) Cosmetic Issues

1. Smile Design/Mock-up
2. Whitener Upper-Lower.
3. Veneers/Crowns _____

IV. What can we expect from treatment?

Musculoskeletal–Occlusal Signs

Exam Form

1. ☐ Headaches

2. ☐ TMJ Pain

3. ☐ TMJ Noise

4. ☐ Limited Opening

5. ☐ Ear Congestion

6. ☐ Vertigo (Dizziness)

7. ☐ Tinnitus (Ringing in the Ears)

8. ☐ Dysphagia (Difficulty Swallowing)

9. ☐ Loose Teeth

10. ☐ Clenching/Bruxing

11. ☐ Facial Pain (Nonspecific)

12. ☐ Tender, Sensitive Teeth (Percussion)

13. ☐ Difficulty Chewing

14. ☐ Cervical Pain

15. ☐ Postural Problems

16. ☐ Paresthesia of Fingertips (Tingling)

17. ☐ Thermal Sensitivity (Hot and Cold)

18. ☐ Trigeminal Neuralgia

19. ☐ Bell's Palsy

20. ☐ Nervousness / Insomnia

SIGNS (Extra-oral)

1. ☐ Facial Asymmetry Bilaterally

2. ☐ Short Lower Third of Face

3. ☐ Chelitis

4. ☐ Abnormal Lip Posture

5. ☐ Deep Mentalis Crease

6. ☐ Dished-Out or Flat Labial Profile

7. ☐ Facial Edema

8. ☐ Mandibular Torticollis

9. ☐ Cervical Torticollis

10. ☐ Lordosis (Forward Head Posture)

11. ☐ Elongated Lower Face (Steep Mandibular Angle)

12. ☐ Speech Abnormalities

SIGNS (Intra-oral)

1. ☐ Crowded Lower Anteriors
2. ☐ Wear of Lower Anterior Teeth
3. ☐ Lingual Inclination of Lower Anteriors
4. ☐ Lingual Inclination of Upper Anteriors (Div II Occusion)
5. ☐ Bicuspid Drop Off
6. ☐ Depressed Curve of Spee
7. ☐ Lingually Tipped Lower Posteriors
8. ☐ Narrow Mandibular Arch
9. ☐ Narrow Maxillary Arch (High Palatal Vault)
10. ☐ Midline Discrepancy
11. ☐ Malrelated Dental Arches
12. ☐ Tooth Mobility
13. ☐ Flared Upper Anterior Teeth
14. ☐ Facets
15. ☐ Cervical Erosion (Abfractions)
16. ☐ Locked Upper Buccal Cusps
17. ☐ Fractured Cusps (Particularly CI. & II Non-functional Cusps)
18. ☐ Chipped Anterior Teeth
19. ☐ Loss of Molars

20. ☐ Open Interproximal Contacts

21. ☐ Unexplained Gingival Inflammation
and Hypertrophy

22. ☐ Crossbite

23. ☐ Anterior Open Bite

24. ☐ Anterior Tongue Thrust

25. ☐ Lateral Tongue Thrust

26. ☐ Scalloping of the Lateral Border of the Tongue

Myotronics-Noromed, Inc.

15425 53rd Avenue South

Tukwila, WV 98188

800. 426.0316 (206)243.4214

Patient Name

Date

SMILE ANALYSIS

1. What bothers you most about your dental appearance?

2. Do you have concerns about:

3. *Spaces / gaps between teeth? If so, where?

4. *Color of teeth?

5. *Size of teeth?

6. *Shape of teeth?

7. *Show too much gum?

8. *Crooked teeth?

9. *Chipped teeth?

10. *Discolored restorations?

Front teeth _____

Back teeth _____

Gums discolored / inflamed?

3. Describe any previous cosmetic treatment:

4. Shimbashi #_____

Existing length of centrals: R _____ L _____

 Desired length _____

Midline and canting: Midline Correct? Yes or No

Midline off? _____ R/L

Axial inclination: correct?

Inclined: labial or lingually

Reverse Smile? Yes or No

Gingival heights okay? Yes or No

Contour needed? _____

"Dr. William Morgan"

"Front-Left: Dr. Mark Britton, Dr. Morgan; Back-Left:
Dr. Dan Anderson, Dr. Ben Stroud, Dr. Joe Griffin"

Laverne and Bill on the train to Paris.

Laverne and Bill on a cruise.

"Morgan-Britton Team" From Left to Right: Dr. Morgan, Pam Kriger, Gwen Lang, Sonya Todd, Amy Vittetoe, Dr. Mark Britton.

"Tennessee Vols Tailgate Pary with Cornerstone Staff"

About the Author

Dr. Morgan is a graduate of the University of Tennessee, College of Dentistry with a degree in Doctor of Dental Surgery. Dr. Morgan received the Fraternal Achievement award for Outstanding Senior. He also holds a B.S. degree from the University of Tennessee, Knoxville.

While serving his country in the United States Navy, Doctor Morgan practiced dentistry until his return to Knoxville in 1968. He worked for Head Start rendering dental care to four-six year old children in Union, Morgan, Anderson and Campbell Counties until he started his private practice in 1970.

Dr. Morgan is a member of the American Dental Association, the Tennessee State Dental Association, the Second District Dental Society and the American Academy of General Dentistry. His post graduate training has been in full mouth reconstruction, TMJ treatment and cosmetic dentistry.

He and his wife, Laverne have three children; Mark, Missy and Brad and eight grandchildren. They are involved in a local Christian church and Laverne has been a leader in Bible Study Fellowship. Dr. Morgan has participated in many medical/dental mission and construction trips to foreign countries.

Credentials
Education:

Purdue University
University of Tennessee, Knoxville
University of Tennesee, UT Medical Units, Memphis
College of Wooster, Ohio
Indiana University
Las Vegas Institute for Advanced Dental Studies

*Member in Good Standing of the
following organizations and societies:*

American Dental Association
Christian Dental Society
Tennessee State Dental Association
Second District Dental Society
American Academy of Cosmetic Dentistry
Academy of General Dentistry
East Tennessee Academy of Dental Practice
Administration
East Tennessee Dental Diagnostic Study Group
Fraternal Organizations
Phi Sigma Alpha–The College of Wooster, Ohio;

Phi Sigma Kappa–University of Tennessee, Knoxville;

Psi Omega–Medical Units, University of Tennessee Memphis

For more information about book orders or to get into contact with him his email is drmorgan@williammorgandds.com; www.williammorgandds.com

Endnotes

1. *This book was written over a span of about four years and that was the number of days per month that I worked then. I only work about eight days per month now as I will explain later in the book. (Pg. 27)

2. * This was several years ago, so those percentages may need to be adjusted to keep up with the market in employee wages. (Percentages given on Pg. 32)

3. * This cruise idea was published in one of Nate's articles along with a picture of my staff and me in the LVI Dental Visions, Volume 11, May/June 2002. If you care to read more about my experiences with LVI, you can find it in August 2003 of LVI Dental Visions with Walter Hailey, the founder of Dental Boot Kamp on the front cover. You can contact LVI for copies of those articles-www.NateBooth.com (Pg. 34)

4. * Outline is on page 100.

5. I heard this first from Jim and Naomi Rhode of SmartPractice Dental. (Pg. 58)

6. * Cornerstone Dental Arts building has 16 operatories. (Pg. 64)

7. *Professional Budget Plan no longer exists. (Pg. 79)

8.　* Mrs. Sue Marshall is a very savvy dental practice coach with great communication skills. She can help you develop a true team. If your team needs help, I highly recommend her. She and her associate Paula Harris, has helped us at Conrerstone Dental Arts. (Pg. 80)

9.　*The number one reason a patient leaves your practice is because a staff member has offended or hurt them. Being able to identify a staff member who is detrimental to your practice is essential. I had a dragon lady hygienist that caused my practice to lose many patients. Keep a pulse on how your patients respond to your staff. (Pg. 82)